A DOLPHIN'S BODY

Bobbie Kalman

🌳 Crabtree Publishing Company

www.crabtreebooks.com

Created by Bobbie Kalman

for my daughter Andrea Crabtree with love

Author and Publisher
Bobbie Kalman

Editorial director
Niki Walker

Editor
Amanda Bishop

Art director
Robert MacGregor

Design
Bobbie Kalman
Campbell Creative Services

Production coordinator
Heather Fitzpatrick

Photo research
Samantha Crabtree
Laura Hysert

Consultant
Patricia Loesche, Ph.D.,
Animal Behavior Program,
Department of Psychology,
University of Washington

Special thanks to:
Diane Sweeney and Dolphin Quest, Lindsey Potter, Marc Crabtree,
and Peter Crabtree

Photographs
© Steve Bloom/stevebloom.com: cover
Photos courtesy of Dolphin Quest Hawaii, located at the Kahala Mandarin
    Oriental Hawaii: title page, pages 9 (right), 13
Bobbie Kalman: title page; taken at Dolphin Quest Hawaii/Hilton Waikoloa
    Village; pages 9 (left), 10 (top), 12, 14 (top), 15 (top); taken at Dolphin
    Quest Hawaii/Kahala Mandarin Oriental Hawaii
John Ford/Vancouver Aquarium Marine Science Centre: page 24
© Phillip Colla/oceanlight.com: page 16 (top)
Marc Crabtree: page 20
© Michael S. Nolan/wildlifeimages.net: pages 14 (bottom), 18, 28,
    29, 31 (top)
Tom Stack & Associates, Inc.: Jeff Foott: page 25 (bottom)
© James D. Watt/wattstock.com: pages 17, 23 (bottom), 25 (top), 30 (left)
Other images by Digital Stock and Digital Vision

Illustrations and artwork:
© Apollo/networlddesign.com/apollo/: pages 4, 19, 26
Barbara Bedell: pages 5 (except beluga and beaked whale), 8, 9, 24, 29
© Ian Coleman/colemangallery.com: pages 21, 22
© Jeff Wilkie/jeffwilkie.com: page 3
Tiffany Wybouw: all borders and decorative dolphins including on back
    cover, pages 5 (beluga and beaked whale), 6-7, 12, 17, 23, 27

Crabtree Publishing Company

www.crabtreebooks.com   1-800-387-7650

PMB 16A	612 Welland Avenue	73 Lime Walk
350 Fifth Avenue	St. Catharines	Headington
Suite 3308	Ontario	Oxford
New York, NY	Canada	OX3 7AD
10118	L2M 5V6	United Kingdom

Cataloging-in-Publication Data
Kalman, Bobbie
  A dolphin's body / Bobbie Kalman.
      p. cm. -- (Dolphin worlds)
Photographs and text provide information on dolphins' physical
characteristics and behavior.
  ISBN 0-7787-1163-3 (RLB) -- ISBN 0-7787-1183-8 (pbk.)
  1. Dolphins--Physiology--Juvenile literature. [1. Dolphins.] I. Title.
QL737.C432 K376 2003
599.53--dc21

LC 2002012080

CONTENTS

WHAT ARE DOLPHINS?

Many people think that dolphins are fish, but dolphins are actually **marine mammals**, or mammals that live in the ocean. Mammals breathe air with lungs, and they are **warm-blooded**. Mammal mothers give birth to live young and **nurse**, or feed their babies, with their own milk.

Dolphins belong to a group of marine mammals called **cetaceans**. The name "cetacean" comes from a Greek word, which means "large sea animal." Cetaceans include whales, dolphins, and porpoises. Some cetaceans, such as the humpback whale shown above, are huge. Next to the whale, the dolphins appear small.

The cetacean family

Cetaceans are divided into two smaller groups—*Mysticeti*, or **baleen whales**, and *Odontoceti*, or **toothed whales**. Baleen whales have hundreds of comblike baleen plates in their mouths. These bony plates have stiff hairs at the ends that filter food from ocean water. The humpback whale on page 4 is a baleen whale.

Toothed whales

Dolphins are toothed whales that catch their food with teeth instead of baleen. Other toothed whales are sperm whales, belugas, narwhals, and beaked whales. Porpoises and river dolphins are also toothed whales. Although some people think these whales are dolphins, they do not belong to the dolphin family.

The sperm whale (top), beluga (left), and beaked whale (right) are toothed whales, but they are not dolphins.

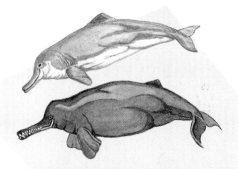

River dolphins such as the baiji (top) and the Ganges River dolphin (bottom) are also toothed whales, but they are not true dolphins.

Porpoises are toothed whales, but they are not dolphins. Most are smaller and stockier than dolphins. They have rounded snouts instead of beaks, and their teeth are spade shaped. Dolphins have cone-shaped teeth.

The dolphins above are true dolphins. To find out which other toothed whales are true dolphins, turn the page!

THE DOLPHIN FAMILY

True dolphins belong to the family Delphinidae. There are 34 to 36 **species**, or types, of true dolphins. Some people are surprised to learn that the family includes pilot whales, melon-headed whales, pygmy killer whales, false killer whales, and orcas. These large dolphins are also known as "blackfish," but they are not fish at all! There are six types of blackfish. They are shown on this page. The largest blackfish—and dolphin—is the orca.

Orcas are also known as killer whales.

All blackfish except the orca, shown below, have a mark on their undersides that resembles a ship's anchor, shown left.

*A long-finned pilot whale has long flippers, a large forehead, and a sloping **dorsal**, or back, fin.*

The short-finned pilot whale has shorter fins and fewer teeth than the long-finned pilot whale has.

The pygmy killer whale eats marine mammals, including other dolphins.

An orca can grow to a length of 32 feet (9.75 m).

The melon-headed whale eats octopus and squid. It lives in warm ocean waters.

The false killer whale is a playful dolphin that loves to approach boats.

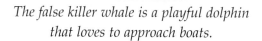

How are they different?

Although dolphins are similar in many ways, there are differences in their sizes, shapes, colors, and behavior. Look at the dolphins on these pages. Notice the various colors, patterns, head and snout shapes, and fin and tail lengths.

Some bottlenose dolphins live in open oceans, some live along coasts, and some even venture into rivers.

Risso's dolphin is a large dolphin that is covered with scars made by the teeth of other Risso's dolphins. It has about ten teeth.

The Indo-Pacific humpback dolphin is a large dolphin with a hump under its dorsal fin.

The southern right whale dolphin has no dorsal fin.

There are long-beaked and short-beaked common dolphins. This is a short-beaked common dolphin.

Spinner dolphins are known for the spectacular spins they make as they leap out of water.

The Atlantic spotted dolphin is born without spots but becomes spotted with age.

Pacific white-sided dolphins are very sociable, even with other dolphin species.

Dusky dolphins are great acrobats. They love to leap! They hunt together in schools.

The small tucuxi lives along coasts and in rivers.

Hector's dolphin is small and very endangered! It has a rounded dorsal fin.

7

ADAPTED TO WATER

The first mammals on Earth lived on land. Some scientists believe that the ancestors of dolphins and whales were four-legged, fur-covered hoofed mammals that shared a common ancestor with the buffalo and hippopotamus. These land-mammal relatives of cetaceans began swimming and fishing in the ocean about 55 million years ago. Slowly, their bodies **adapted**, or changed, until the animals needed to live in water full time.

Over millions of years, the ancestors **evolved** into other types of animals, such as those shown below. Their nostrils became **blowholes** and moved to the top of their heads. Gradually, they lost their fur and grew a thick layer of **blubber**, or fat, to keep them warm in water. Their front feet became flippers, their necks grew shorter and stiffer, and their back legs disappeared. Their tails changed into **flukes**. About 10 to 12 million years ago, dolphins became a unique group of marine mammals.

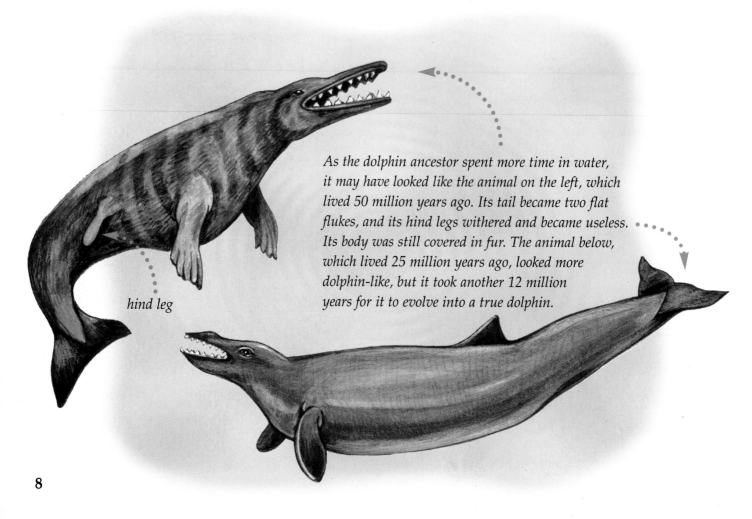

hind leg

As the dolphin ancestor spent more time in water, it may have looked like the animal on the left, which lived 50 million years ago. Its tail became two flat flukes, and its hind legs withered and became useless. Its body was still covered in fur. The animal below, which lived 25 million years ago, looked more dolphin-like, but it took another 12 million years for it to evolve into a true dolphin.

Dolphin bodies became smooth and **streamlined**, or sleek, allowing the animals to slip easily through water.

If you look at an X-ray of a dolphin flipper, you can see "finger" bones through its skin. A dolphin ancestor once had hands similar to ours. In the picture below, the bones are visible through the skin of the dolphin's flipper.

A dolphin's flukes have no bones. They are made of tough, fatty material that feels like rubber.

Dolphins are mammals like you and me, but their bodies are perfectly suited to living and moving in water. Water **resists**, or pushes against, objects that move in it (see page 16). When we swim or dive, water resists our noses, arms, legs, and ears because they stick out. This makes us move slowly. The streamlined shape and smooth skin of dolphins allow them to glide effortlessly through water without much resistance. The long, powerful bodies of dolphins can move much faster in water than our bodies can.

Dolphins shed their outer skin cells every two to three hours to help keep their skin shiny smooth. Humans shed their skin cells only about once a day.

A dolphin's thin skin is easily cut, scratched, and sunburned. Without water, a dolphin's skin would dry out quickly, and its body would overheat.

*The powerful muscles in the **peduncle**, or tail stock, move the dolphin's flukes up and down.*

Tail flukes propel the dolphin forward.

Did you know that dolphins have belly buttons? Before a dolphin is born, it is attached to its mother by an umbilical cord. After birth, the mother breaks the cord with her teeth. The rest of the cord falls off a few days later, leaving only a tiny "button."

Dark back, light belly

A dolphin's body has **countershading**, which means it is darker on top than it is on the bottom. Countershading helps **camouflage** dolphins. If you look at a dolphin from below, its light abdomen blends in with the sunlit ocean surface. From above, the dolphin's gray or black back blends in with the dark, deep waters below the dolphin.

The dorsal fin keeps the dolphin balanced and also helps release heat from its body. The fin is made of the same material as that found in the flukes.

A dolphin's ears do not stick out and slow the dolphin down as it swims. They are tiny holes behind the eyes.

A dolphin breathes through a blowhole at the top of its head.

A dolphin's beak is called a **rostrum**.

The two **pectoral fins**, or flippers, help the dolphin steer as it moves through water.

A dolphin sheds oily tears to protect its eyes underwater.

LOOK INSIDE!

Like all mammals, a dolphin is a **vertebrate**. A vertebrate has a **spinal column**, or backbone. A skeleton made up of bones supports the dolphin's body and protects organs such as a heart and liver, lungs, kidneys, and intestines. The illustration below shows the inside of a dolphin's body.

Some of a dolphin's body parts are different from those of a land mammal because everything inside this marine mammal is suited to life in water. A dolphin's skeleton, for example, does not have to be as strong as that of a land mammal. A land mammal supports its body weight with its bones, but water supports the weight of a dolphin's body.

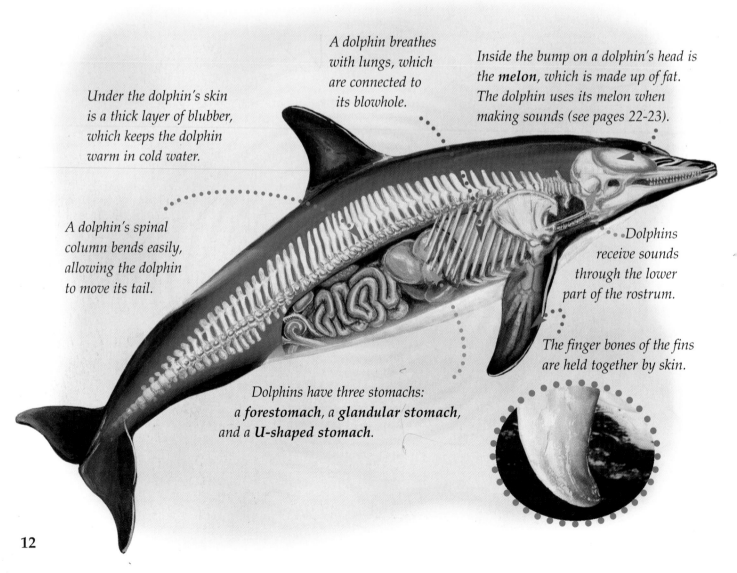

A dolphin breathes with lungs, which are connected to its blowhole.

*Inside the bump on a dolphin's head is the **melon**, which is made up of fat. The dolphin uses its melon when making sounds (see pages 22-23).*

Under the dolphin's skin is a thick layer of blubber, which keeps the dolphin warm in cold water.

A dolphin's spinal column bends easily, allowing the dolphin to move its tail.

Dolphins receive sounds through the lower part of the rostrum.

The finger bones of the fins are held together by skin.

*Dolphins have three stomachs: a **forestomach**, a **glandular stomach**, and a **U-shaped stomach**.*

Teeth for grabbing

Dolphins have between four and 252 identical cone-shaped teeth, which are ideal for grabbing slippery prey. They do not lose their teeth, which appear a few weeks after birth. They keep them throughout their lives. Dolphins do not chew their food. They swallow it whole or tear it into chunks and then swallow it. Dolphins also do not drink water. They get all the water they need from the food they eat.

Down the hatch!

A dolphin's food passes through three stomachs after it is swallowed. First, the food goes into the fore-stomach, which acts as a storage chamber. Next, it passes into the dolphin's glandular stomach, or "true" stomach, which contains digestive chemicals that break down food. The food then goes into the U-shaped stomach, which ends in a strong muscle that regulates the flow of food to the small intestines. The small intestine absorbs nutrients from the food and passes the waste to the large intestine, which carries it out of the body. The intestines are shown in the diagram on page 12. They are the sausage-like organs.

VOLUNTARY BREATHING

Unlike fish, dolphins cannot breathe underwater. They have lungs, like all mammals, which means they need to breathe air. Dolphins must come to the water's surface to breathe. As they break the surface, they exhale and blow out huge blasts of warm air. The breaths are loud and accompanied by mists of water droplets, which shoot into the air. The mist is created when the warm air from a dolphin's lungs meets the cold air and the water droplets around the blowhole. Before diving again, a dolphin takes a breath and closes its blowhole with a special muscle plug, shown in the picture on the left.

The dolphin knows when to open its blowhole by sensing air around it. It can empty and refill its lungs in a fifth of a second. The air leaves its blowhole at a speed of up to 22 miles per hour (36 km/h).

Not mouth breathers

A dolphin's blowhole is connected only to the animal's lungs and not to its mouth or stomach. This adaptation is useful in two ways. A dolphin can eat underwater without taking water into its lungs. At the surface, it can eat and breathe at the same time, and it will not choke.

Half asleep

Unlike humans, who do not have to think about breathing, dolphins are **voluntary breathers**. Voluntary breathers must make a conscious effort to breathe, even while they are sleeping. Since dolphins must remind themselves to breathe, they cannot have deep sleeps. Instead, they take short naps near the surface of the ocean and slowly rise to take a breath. While they sleep, they keep one eye open and close the other. Scientists think that dolphins shut off one half of their brains when they rest and keep the other half awake enough to breathe. When dolphins are half asleep, they are also half awake!

Less rest

People need more sleep than dolphins do! Land animals are easily tired because their bodies must support their body weight against the pull of gravilty. Dolphins do not need as much rest because water supports their body weight. They need only short naps, whereas people need about eight hours of sleep each night!

You can tell this dolphin is sleeping because its eye is closed, and it is floating on the surface of the water.

*Dolphins often rest in tight groups to protect themselves from **predators**. These spotted dolphins are "rafting" just below the ocean's surface. They float up to breathe.*

15

 # BODIES IN MOTION

(top) Dolphins can move at high speeds. (above) Calves usually swim under their mothers' fins. Above water, they struggle to keep up with their mothers.

Dolphins are so well suited to water that they can move through it quickly with little effort. When anything moves through water, it creates **drag**. Drag is a force that slows down movement. It is created mainly by **friction**, or the rubbing of water as it flows over and around a moving body. A dolphin's stream-lined shape helps reduce drag by allowing water to flow smoothly over the dolphin's body. Its pectoral fins act as **hydrofoils**. Hydrofoils are shaped like the wings of birds and airplanes, but they work in water rather than in air. Water flows over and under the fins and creates **lift**, which keeps dolphins from sinking, so they do not have to work hard to move through water.

How a dolphin moves

A dolphin propels itself forward by moving its tail and flukes up and down in water. The upward movement of the tail is called a **power stroke**, and the downward movement is known as the **recovery stroke**. Until recently, scientists did not think that the recovery stroke propelled the dolphin, but some now think that it also moves the dolphin forward.

As dolphins move their tails up and down, their bodies bend and curve in the opposite direction. They move forward and down with the power stroke. They move upward with the recovery stroke. As a result, dolphins do not swim in straight lines but, instead, swim in curving paths. They usually come to the surface at the top of each curve and take a breath before moving down again.

*When the **dorsal**, or backside, muscles contract, they move the tail upward in the power stroke.*

*When the **ventral**, or underside, muscles contract, they pull the tail downward for the recovery stroke.*

The tail then comes up again and moves the dolphin down and forward in a curving path.

Talented acrobats

Dolphins swim upward, downward, and upside down. They dive, leap, and **porpoise**, or move quickly forward by leaping out of the water (see picture on page 18). Spinner dolphins are named after the spectacular spins they make as they leave the water. You can see water droplets circling this dolphin as it spins.

17

MOVING AND DIVING

Most dolphins do not **migrate**, or travel very far from where they live, but they are constantly on the move. How do dolphins know where they are going? In shallow water and at the surface, they watch for landmarks, but there are no landmarks in deep waters. Dolphins may be able to find their way in the open ocean by using **geomagnetic sensitivity**. Scientists think that a dolphin's brain contains tiny crystals of **iron oxide**, or **magnetite**. These crystals react to the Earth's magnetic field in the same way a compass does. They may allow the dolphin to "read" the magnetic field and know in which direction it is traveling, but no one is really sure how a dolphin finds its way.

When groups of dolphins go their separate ways, they seem to know where to meet up again, even without landmarks to tell them which way to swim.

Going down!

Dolphins can dive deep and hold their breath for up to fifteen minutes because their bodies use oxygen more efficiently than the bodies of land mammals do. Dolphins can expand their lungs to hold a large amount of air because their rib cages are very flexible. They use up to 90 percent of their lung capacity and can store oxygen in their blood and muscles until they need it. We use only 10 to 15 percent of our lung capacity when we breathe, and our blood and organs do not store very much oxygen.

To conserve oxygen, dolphins can shut down all their organs except their hearts and brains. They can even reduce their heart rates to use less oxygen!

DOLPHIN SENSES

Just as a dolphin's body is well suited to the water, so are its senses. Dolphins have excellent hearing and vision and a highly developed sense of touch.

The importance of touch

Dolphins use touch to learn more about their surroundings. Their skin contains a complex system of nerves that can sense heat and the movement of ocean currents. Dolphins also use touch in another way. They use it to strengthen their bonds with other dolphins (see page 30).

Can dolphins taste?

Like humans, dolphins have taste buds on their tongues, and they can tell if something is bitter, sweet, sour, or salty. Tastes give them information about their environment.

Do they have a sense of smell?

A sense of smell is not very useful in water, so it is not likely that dolphins are able to smell. A dolphin's blowhole opens only above water, so it could not smell anything underwater, and dolphin brains have no **smell receptors**, or cells that recognize smell.

Seeing above and below water

Dolphins can see well both above and below water. Strong muscles around their eyes allow them to move their eyeballs around to see ahead as well as to the sides. Dolphins can even move each eye in a different direction! Not only do dolphins have moveable eyeballs, but they also have stretchy pupils that can focus on objects near and far as well. Dolphins can also open their pupils wide underwater to let in more light and close them down to slits above water to shut out bright sunshine.

Excellent hearing

Even though dolphins have no external ears, they can hear extremely well both underwater and above the ocean's surface. Sounds such as those made by approaching animals or by raindrops hitting the ocean's surface help dolphins receive information about their environment. Most scientists believe that sound travels to a dolphin's inner ear through its jaw. A dolphin's ear canal is separated by foam-filled air spaces that keep out unnecessary noises.

Painting by Ian Coleman www.colemangallery.com

Excellent senses of sight and hearing give dolphins information about their environment. These dolphins can hear and sense the fish behind them. The dolphins at the bottom of the picture are using another special sense that very few animals have. Turn the page to find out what it is!

Painting by Ian Coleman www.colemangallery.com

A DOLPHIN SUPERSENSE

All dolphins, along with some other toothed whales, use a special system of "seeing and hearing" called **echolocation**. Echolocation means creating sounds and using their echoes to investigate the surrounding environment or to locate objects. Dolphins have special fatty deposits in their melons and lower jaws that allow them to send and receive sounds. A dolphin creates clicking sounds in the nasal passages below its blowhole and uses its melon to focus the sounds in the direction of an object. It varies the loudness of the clicks, depending on the noise in its environment and the distance of the object it is trying to locate. The clicks come into contact with the object, and the dolphin feels the echoes as they bounce back. The echoes travel from the dolphin's jaw to its middle ear, inner ear, and finally, to its brain. The brain interprets the echoes and constructs a "sound picture."

How echolocation works

When using echolocation, a dolphin first sends out and receives a series of clicks to learn more about its environment. If the echoes of the clicks tell the dolphin there is an object ahead, the dolphin sends out a series of more rapid clicks. These rapid clicks and their echoes give the dolphin details about the size, shape, and location of the object. A final round of clicks and echoes tells the dolphin the object's exact location. The dolphins on these pages are all using echolocation to find food under the sand.

clicks sent out from the melon

echoes received through the rostrum

This spotted dolphin is digging into the sand for a fish it has located. Some scientists believe that dolphins may also use echolocation to stun fish.

HAVING BABIES

Male and female dolphins **mate** in order to **reproduce**, or have babies. Females can start having babies, called **calves**, at around the age of six years, but many do not have them until much later. Although dolphins have only one calf at a time, they can have many offspring because they live a long time. After mating, the males leave and do not take part in raising their young. A calf **gestates**, or grows inside its mother, for ten to thirteen months. When it is ready to be born, it **emerges** tail first so that its blowhole comes out last and the calf does not drown. As soon as it is born, the calf must swim quickly to the surface of the water to breathe. The dolphin mother or another adult helper lifts the calf out of the water so it can take its first breath. The calf needs to breathe often because its small lungs cannot hold much air. A mother is very protective of her calf, which swims under her fin or at her side, where it can nurse easily. The calf is pulled along by the water moving past the mother's body. Even after a calf is fully grown, it stays with its mother for up to six years.

This orca calf is emerging tail first from its mother. The birth is taking place at an aquarium. Very few people have witnessed a dolphin birth in the wild!

This spotted dolphin calf is nursing as it swims along with its mother. Most calves nurse for two years, but some nurse until they are adults.

Mother's milk

A mother's **mammary glands**, which make milk, are along the walls of her chest. Her nipples are inside two slits near her tail. Calves nurse every fifteen minutes, but only for fifteen seconds at a time.

A mother dolphin squeezes her muscles to squirt milk into her calf's mouth so the calf will not need to hold its breath for very long. The milk is high in fat and protein and makes the baby grow quickly. It also helps the calf grow a thick layer of blubber.

This orca baby looks like its mother, but some dolphin calves have coloring that is different from that of their mothers.

25

INTELLIGENT ANIMALS

There is more to dolphins than the parts that make up their bodies. Dolphins are intelligent, and there are many things they can do that other animals cannot. Dolphins enjoy being in the company of other dolphins. They are social animals that are constantly making decisions about interacting with others. They communicate with one another using sounds and body language. They play together and cooperate in finding food. They make choices and need to be able to trust others with whom they swim, rest, and hunt.

Could that be me?

One of the signs of high intelligence is self-recognition and self-awareness. Dolphins are able to recognize themselves in mirrors and know that they are distinct individuals. Humans and apes are the only other animals shown to have this ability. Captive dolphins can perform complex tasks and are capable of memorizing long routines. They also seem to have a sense of humor and often surprise their trainers.

The bubbles made by these orcas may mean that they are making sounds. Could these dolphins be speaking "Orcanese?"

"Here I am!"

A dolphin uses a **signature whistle**, or name, to identify itself to the members of its group. It announces, "Here I am!" by whistling its "name." If a dolphin wants to call another dolphin by name, it will **mimic**, or imitate, his or her whistle. A mother whistles to her baby constantly so that the calf learns her name. The baby also develops its own whistle name.

Do you speak Dolphinese?

Dolphins use body language to communicate information such as direction or the location of prey. They may also have a language based on sounds, but humans have not yet been able to learn it. Besides the sounds that humans can hear, dolphins also make many sounds that are beyond the hearing of humans. Humans might not be able to understand dolphin language, but dolphins grasp some parts of human language with ease.

Able to learn sign language

When researchers taught dolphins sign language, they found that the dolphins learned it quickly and easily. Not only did a group of trained dolphins learn the meanings of more than 60 words, but they also understood sentences. They could follow directions given to them, even when they were not familiar with a new sentence command. The dolphins were also able to follow directions on a video monitor. Most animals would think of the monitor as an object, but the dolphins actually watched what was on the screen and understood that directions were being given to them in a different way.

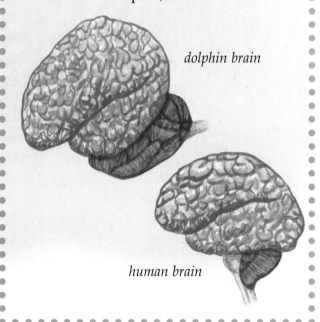

Big brains

A dolphin's brain looks similar to a human brain, but it is quite different. Much of a dolphin's brain is used to interpret echolocation information. The most intelligent dolphin, with the largest brain for its size, is the bottlenose dolphin, shown above.

dolphin brain

human brain

DaNGeRoUS WaTeRS

Dolphins may seem playful and carefree, but they face many dangers in the oceans. They suffer from all kinds of diseases and are plagued by **parasites**. The spinner dolphin in the picture above is being attacked by a remora, a parasitic fish that has damaged the skin on the dolphin's throat. Remoras have suckers on their mouths that cling to the bodies of spinners. Scientists believe that these dolphins may spin to dislodge the pesky parasites. Parasites cannot always be seen, however. More dangerous parasites, such as hookworms, lung mites, and tapeworms, live inside dolphins' bodies. These internal parasites can cause weakness and even death. Dolphins also suffer from pneumonia, heart disease, and other diseases that can spread quickly among dolphin populations. Dolphins are an **indicator species**. They reflect the health of oceans. Whatever affects them will affect the health of other marine creatures as well as animals in other parts of the world. Poor dolphin health is a warning that all creatures, including people, are in trouble.

Poisoned by pollution

Many diseases are new to dolphins, and scientists think that pollution is to blame. Chemicals in the water are absorbed by fish, which are then eaten by dolphins. Dolphins are slowly poisoned by the many chemicals in the oceans. Their **immune systems** are weakened, and they cannot fight off diseases. Dolphin calves are especially at risk. The poisons are stored in a dolphin's fat. Dolphin milk is mostly fat, so a calf gets a dose of poison from its mother's milk each time it nurses. Many calves die before they are a year old. Human diseases have also begun to show up in dolphins, possibly from human sewage that is washed into the oceans.

People—enemies and friends

Thousands of dolphins are killed each year in fishing nets. In some places, dolphins are still hunted for food. Dolphins are also killed by motorboats and undersea noise from boats and navy **sonar**. Sonar equipment produces sounds similar to the echolocation sounds of dolphins. A new kind of sonar, called **LFAS**, or **Low Frequency Active Sonar**, is very loud and dangerous to all cetaceans. During tests of LFAS, dead whales and dolphins with ear, lung, and brain damage washed up on shorelines. Although some people hurt dolphins, many work hard to save them. You can help dolphins, too, by learning more about what you can do to help them.

Try these excellent websites

www.cetacea.org   www.dolphinsmiles.com
www.bluevoice.org   www.dolphinproject.org
www.friendsoftheocean.org   www.cmc-ocean.org
www.animaltime.net/dolphins
www.artfuldolphin.com/thedolphins

Shark attack!

Many people think that there are no sharks where dolphins swim, but sharks attack dolphins all the time! Large sharks, such as bull sharks, tiger sharks, and makos, prey on young and sick dolphins. Another shark, called the cookie cutter shark, often injures dolphins. This tiny shark, which ranges in size from 6 to 20 inches (15-51 cm), is able to unhinge its jaws, attach onto a victim, and cut out a perfectly round plug of flesh, as shown on the right.

FASCINATING BODY FACTS

Staying in touch

Dolphins have very sensitive skin and seem to enjoy being touched. Touching is also a way that dolphins relate to one another. Dolphins are social animals, and most belong to groups. Groups cooperate in finding food and hunting. Touching helps dolphins get to know members of their groups. Mother dolphins touch their babies often to make them feel secure.

Small differences

Many baby dolphins are chubby versions of their mothers. They have large heads and stocky bodies. Some are a different color or have different patterns than those of their mothers.

"Fin"tastic!

You can tell an orca by its fin! Most orcas are easy to recognize in the water because of their huge sizes, but did you know that they also have differently shaped fins? Male orcas, shown right, have straight fins that can be more than six feet (1.8 m) tall. Female orcas have smaller, curved fins, as shown below.

How many spots?

You can tell whether an Atlantic spotted dolphin is young or old by the number of spots on its skin. Baby spotted dolphins have very few spots, but the older they get, the more spots they will have. Not all spotted dolphins are covered in spots, however. Some have only a few, even at an older age.

Candle jumps

After eating a large meal, some dolphins jump straight up out of the water and then fall back in the same position. Scientists believe that these jumps may help settle the meal in a dolphin's stomach. The jumps are called "candles," probably because the dolphins look a bit like candles when they are in this position.

GLOSSARY

Note: Boldfaced words that are defined in the book may not appear in the glossary

camouflage Colors and patterns on an animal's fur or skin that allow it to blend in with its environment

cetaceans A group of marine mammals, including dolphins, that have nearly hairless bodies, wide front flippers, and flat tails

emerge To come out or appear

evolve To change gradually over time

friction The rubbing together of two objects when one or both are moving

geomagnetic sensitivity The ability to read the magnetic field of the Earth to orient oneself

indicator species A species whose presence or absence in an environment shows the conditions of that environment, such as high levels of pollution

immune system The parts of a body that work together to fight illness

LFAS Low Frequency Active Sonar; very loud and dangerous sound waves produced by navy sonar equipment that hurt or kill ocean creatures

magnetite A mineral found in the brains of some animals that helps them find direction

mate To join together to make babies

migrate To travel long distances to find food, reproduce, or enjoy better weather conditions

parasite An organism that lives off another

predator An animal that hunts other animals for food

species Within a larger group of animals, a smaller group with similar bodies that are able to make babies together

voluntary breathing Breathing that requires an animal to inhale and exhale consciously

warm-blooded Describing an animal with a body temperature that does not change with its surroundings

INDEX

1 2 3 4 5 6 7 8 9 0   Printed in the U.S.A.   2 1 0 9 8 7 6 5 4 3